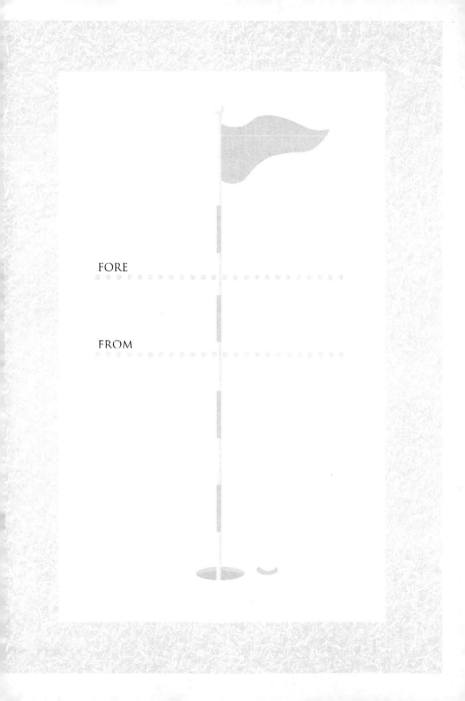

FORE

FROM

HOW TO
REALLY
STINK
AT GOLF

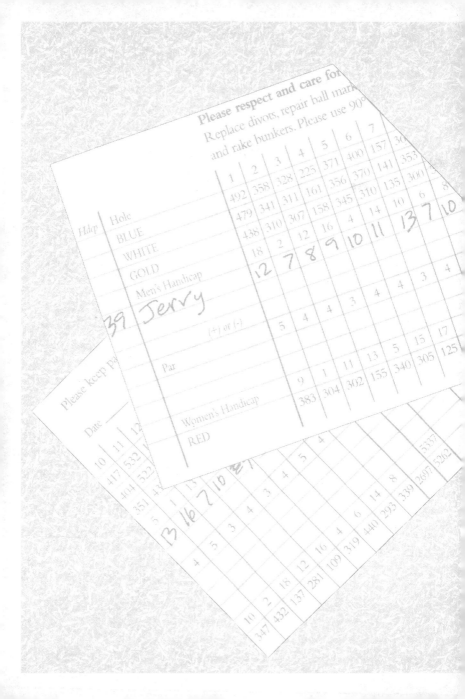

HOW TO REALLY STINK AT GOLF

Jeff Foxworthy
& Brian Hartt

Illustrations by
Layron DeJarnette

VILLARD ⓥ NEW YORK

Published in the United States by Villard Books, an imprint of
The Random House Publishing Group, a division of
Random House, Inc., New York.

VILLARD and "V" CIRCLED Design are registered trademarks of
Random House, Inc.

Library of Congress Cataloging-in-Publication Data

Foxworthy, Jeff.
How to really stink at golf / Jeff Foxworthy & Brian Hartt.
p.   cm.
ISBN 978-0-345-50278-0
1. Golf—Humor.   I. Hartt, Brian.   II. Title.
PN6231.G68F69 2008
818'.5402—dc22   2008004926

Printed in the United States of America on acid-free paper

www.villard.com

2 4 6 8 9 7 5 3 1

First Edition

Book design by Susan Turner

Dedicated to John Hartt

—B.H.

PREFACE

They say the first step toward dealing with any problem is to admit that you do, in fact, have a problem. In this case it's your golf game and, quite honestly, it stinks.

There are things you can do to correct this problem. You could pay for expensive lessons and make endless trips to the range to practice. But that is time-consuming and will probably be fruitless in the end.

Besides, if you did become good at golf, think of the added pressure it would bring to your life. You'd have to travel to tournaments all the time, which would take you away from your family. Every morning you'd have to rush out and get the paper to see where you stood in the world rankings. You'd have to create a space in your closet for a green jacket that you'd never wear anywhere. It would just be a constant hassle.

So, with that in mind, embrace the fact that you do stink at golf.

Relieve yourself of the stress of breaking 70 or 80 or 90 or even 100. Do the things that will assure you that not only do you stink now, but you will really stink for the rest of your life. That, my friend, is an inner peace that surpasses all understanding.

CONTENTS

HOW TO
REALLY
STINK
AT GOLF

PREGAME RITUALS

L ike anything worthwhile in life, a bad round of golf needs a solid foundation. If you're a drinker, a hangover and two hours of sleep is a good place to start.

If you don't drink, there are other things you can do to lay down a good foundation for a bad round of golf. Like eating at a Mexican restaurant that's received a score of 58 from the board of health. This will add not only discomfort but also a sense of urgency to your round. And it opens the door to creating a story that your buddies will tell for years to come.

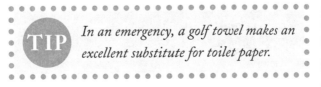

TIP *In an emergency, a golf towel makes an excellent substitute for toilet paper.*

"You owe me a towel, Jerry!"

DON'T WARM UP

Try to get to the golf course right at your tee time. This way you can avoid the hassle of warming up.

My theory is that you're only going to hit five good shots in the course of the day, so why waste one on the driving range? Isn't it better to start playing right away, rather than embarrassing yourself in front of yet more people? Of course it is.

And whatever you do, don't stretch. You might pull something.

HOW TO SCREW UP A
GREAT DRIVE

It's one of the greatest feelings in the world. People are watching. The pressure's on. And you smack a drive straight and long down the middle of the fairway.

Now: Time to screw it up!

As you walk to your ball, keep telling yourself, "Don't screw up your drive." If you're already talking to yourself on the second shot of the day, it's a bad sign. And that's good. And since the next shot is such an important one, you're going to want to see where it goes right away. So as you swing through the ball, lift your head.

Hey, you may even hear yourself scream, "I lifted my head!" as your ball sails dead left with the arc of a banana. Congratulations, my friend: You've set the table for another horrible round of golf.

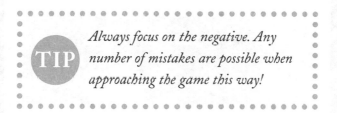

TIP *Always focus on the negative. Any number of mistakes are possible when approaching the game this way!*

THE GOLF CART

Try to pick a cart that looks like it's been through a war. Because with your game, it's sure to have to go off-road at some point. If it barely has enough juice to make it up the first hill, whatever you do, don't turn around and exchange it for a better cart. This would not only eliminate stress from your day, it would rob you of a primo excuse for your crappy round later on.

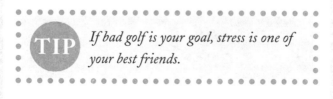

TIP *If bad golf is your goal, stress is one of your best friends.*

14

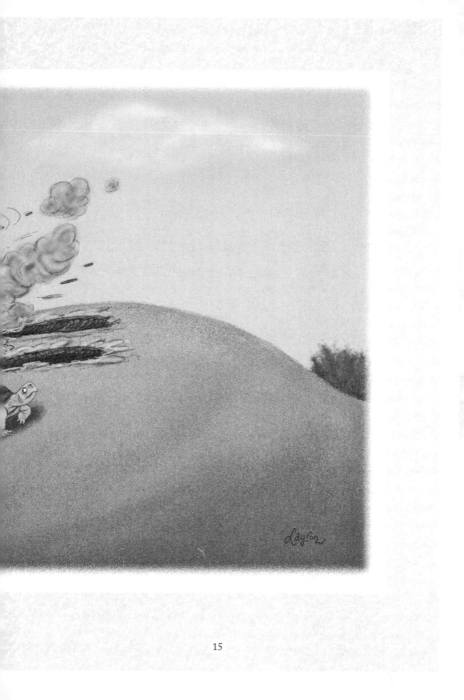

TREES

When you wind up in the trees (and you will), DO NOT PLAY IT SAFE! That's what the trees want you to do. They want you to look bad. Don't let them win. If you've sliced the ball into a forest but can still see an inch of daylight through some branches fifty yards away, GO FOR IT!

If Tiger Woods can make this shot one time in a thousand, why can't you? Remember, many a scorecard adventure has begun with the words "Hand me my two-iron, I'm going to try to blast it out of here."

Don't punch the ball onto the fairway until you've tried every possible way out. If your buddies aren't hiding behind a cart, you haven't tried hard enough. If you wimp out here, you'll never know the glory of what might have been!

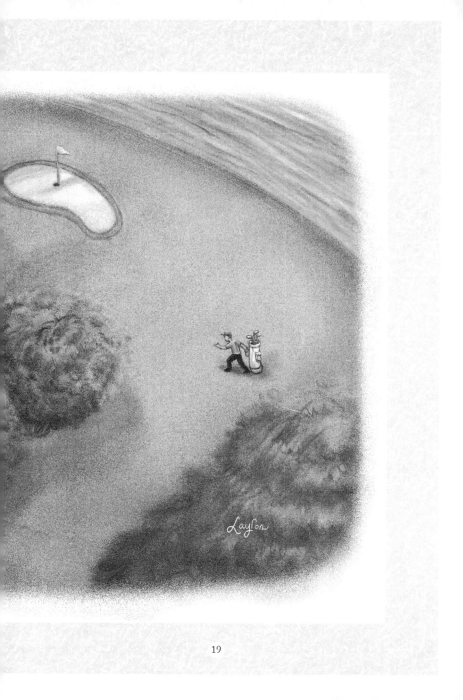

AVOID FUN

I n the mysterious world of golf there are evil forces at work that will keep you from having a bad round. And one of the most powerful of these is "having fun."

Avoid fun. Fun is for children. And otters. This is serious. Why? . . . I don't know. But it is. It just is.

FUN = RELAXED = LOW SCORES

. . . and that's something we want to avoid.

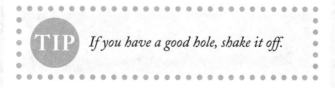

TIP *If you have a good hole, shake it off.*

"Quit staring at me, Jerry!"

PLAYING PARTNERS

It has been said that in golf you're not playing against anybody else, you're playing against the course. Baloney! That kind of silly thinking eliminates way too much stress. You are playing against everyone in your group, so you should maniacally study the scorecard after every hole and calculate how many strokes you need to need to make up. This way you can make smart decisions like going for it from 278 yards out with a water hazard between you and the hole.

As we've discussed, it's next to impossible to really stink at golf without stress. So you should select the group you're playing with carefully.

Here are some promising foursomes:

You

Your sex-crazed single buddy with the great stories

Your friend with the filthiest mouth on the planet

Your preacher

. . . .

You

Your friend who just got out of rehab

A stranger who really needs to go to rehab

Your mother

. . . .

You

Your wife

Your ex-wife

Your girlfriend

"Hit the #@%* out of it, preacher!!!"

PAR 5'S

It's impossible to resist the temptation of going for birdie on a par 5. So when stepping up to the tee on these long, majestic holes, have only one thought on your mind: KILL THE BALL!

Kill it! Hit it as hard as you can! After all, the harder you hit something, the farther it goes, right? That's just scientific fact, right? So whack it with all your might, then sit back and watch the magic.

Now, if, for some strange reason, your ball doesn't go very far, you'll have ground to make up. So . . . KILL IT AGAIN! Use your driver off the fairway if you have to! Keep killing it till you eventually get to the hole. If you're not making an audible noise, you're not swinging hard enough.

THE CART GIRL

To stink at golf on a consistent basis you need distractions, and plenty of them. One of the best is a gorgeous cart girl with a great personality. You won't have time to keep your head down as you scan the horizon, looking for any sign that she might be headed back your way.

Think about it: As a stunning twenty-two-year-old, she'd be crazy not to want to hook up with an out-of-shape old married guy with goofy plaid pants and a sunburned nose! Come on, there's no way she's not checkin' you out as you pop a heart pill and change your glasses while lining up a two-foot putt for an 8.

Why don't you save the heart attack for after you miss a birdie on the eighteenth green, blowing your shot at breaking 80?

ALCOHOL

I f you have a problem with alcohol, now is not the time to try to control it. Slowed reflexes and distorted judgment can only work to your benefit if you really want to stink at golf.

Besides, downing a few cool ones almost guarantees you'll make an off-color comment about a playing partner's wife or girlfriend, and that'll open the door for anger and tension. If one of your playing partners happens to be your boss, you might lose your job. Which, of course, would give you plenty of free time to play more golf.

TIP *Drinking also helps with getting over great tragedies and makes you funny at parties.*

YOUR CELL PHONE

Whatever you do, don't turn your cell phone off. That next call "could be the one"!

Plus, this is the age of multitasking. You can play golf, conduct business, and argue with your sister about whether or not to place your mother in a home, all at the same time.

Don't cheat by putting your cell on vibrate. What could be better than if, as your buddy's putting for his first par in fifty holes, he hears "What's up, doc?!" blaring from your pocket?

> **TIP** *Good shot-wrecking ringtones are: chain saws, bagpipes, Aerosmith, Gomer Pyle saying "Go-olly!," and any ray-gun sound.*

GUESSING WHAT CLUB TO USE

We're not pros, so we don't have genius caddies who spend hours mapping out every club selection from every part of the course. No! We have to do the hard work ourselves. And if you pick the wrong club, it could be the difference between a hole in one or winding up in the sand! That's why it's imperative that you second-guess every guess you guess.

Here's what I do from 140 yards out:

1. Stand there for a really long time just looking off.

2. Pull out my eight-iron.

3. Line up the ball and take a few practice swings.

4. Ask Jerry what club I should use.

5. Tell Jerry I don't have a nine-wood.

6. Second-guess my eight-iron and go back and get my seven-iron. But as soon as I pull it out, second-guess my seven-iron and decide to go with my eight-iron once again.

7. Tell Jerry to quit talking to the cart girl while I'm trying to concentrate.

8. As I swing through the ball, think only about how I've made a STUPID CHOICE and should be using my seven-iron.

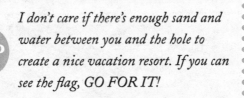

TIP

I don't care if there's enough sand and water between you and the hole to create a nice vacation resort. If you can see the flag, GO FOR IT!

SO, YOU WANT TO BREAK A CLUB

To get to the point where you would actually smash your pitching wedge on a ball washer or wrap your putter around a tree, you must exclude all prejudices, including:

A. how much it cost

B. if it was a gift

C. if your fiancée's father is watching

Once that's out of the way, remember one thing: It's not you. You're not the problem. Your STUPID CLUB has just missed an easy shot, and therefore it must be destroyed. Why must you keep suffering? You, who have lugged it around and cleaned it and put all your confidence in it. And it goes and does THIS!

There . . .

Now you're putting with a five-iron. Until you break it.

By the time you're teeing off with your ball retriever, the high score you're looking for is all but guaranteed.

FAIRWAYS

Fairways mean short grass and level lies. Avoid them like the plague. The golfer who consistently plays off the fairway is in constant danger of recording low scores. And that, my friend, is a no-no.

It is easy to hit a ball from the fairway. And you've never taken the easy way out. They call it the "rough" for a reason. Sissies don't like it rough. But you do!

As you stand on a sidehill lie staring down at the top of a ball buried in five inches of grass, yell to the greenskeeper, "Is that all you've got?!" Then laugh like a madman and start chopping!

LOST BALLS

It has always been my belief that one of the most frustrating things about being a bad golfer is losing expensive golf balls. That's why I quit doing it. Oh, I still lose golf balls by the dozens; they're just not expensive. They're free!

While you're in the woods searching for your errant drive, take the time to look around for other lost balls. If they're scuffed or discolored, who cares? You're gonna lose them again anyway.

Water hazards are a great place to find golf balls. That's why they put them there: to suck in your golf balls so they can pay a kid five bucks to retrieve them and then they can sell them back to you! Well, not me. What do they think I am, an idiot? I don't care if I have to get naked. I'm grabbing not only my lost ball but every other ball I can pick up with my toes.

If you do these things not only will you guarantee yourself the ability to continue to stink by using damaged and malformed balls, you're also sure to make the group behind you blind with rage at how slow you're playing, which will lead to long-distance cuss fights, resulting in extreme elevations in your blood pressure, which is essential to your target goal: another bad round of golf.

SWING THOUGHTS

Before you get set to address the ball, you should have some "swing thoughts" prepared—and plenty of them.

These are my inner thoughts as I'm setting up to swing:

"Feet shoulder width apart, relax at the knees, arms straight, hands forming a perfect V, remember to rotate your hips, not too fast on the takeaway, are your shoes tied? Yeah, I'm pretty sure they are, check the wind, did I leave the stove on this morning? Keep your head down, I wonder if everybody is watching me, this is taking too long, I should just back off, relax, and start over. Nah. I'm okay. Take a deep breath, eye on the ball, I can see Jerry out of the corner of my eye, I hope I don't hit him, I wish that cart girl would come back soon, la la la dee dee dee doo, I wonder why my left arm is numb, SWING!!!!!"

Obviously, your particular pattern may vary, but this one has been proven time and again to put me in the perfect mental space to shank one dead left into the woods.

BAD WEATHER

If your game is horrible in perfect conditions, just think of what you can accomplish in the face of a natural disaster. Besides, if God hadn't wanted you to play in a torrential downpour, he wouldn't have invented the rain suit. In addition, I've found that mud on half the ball creates flight patterns that would amaze NASA. Hey, if you have to approach the green on the dry side of the hole, it's a great day for golf!

An added bonus is that water does flow downhill, so there's a good chance your putt could be washed away from the hole. (When this happens, see "Swearing," page 66.)

Don't forget to play in intense heat at every

opportunity. For example, if you're playing in Phoenix in July, try to get a twelve o'clock tee time. When your kidneys shut down at two-thirty, your 14 strokes on a par 3 will be the least of your concerns.

Cold weather is also good. You were never comfortable with your grip anyway, so not being able to feel your hands shouldn't really matter. Besides, when you skull an iron shot, the pain that shoots up your arms will give you something to talk about other than why they don't make down-filled golf shoes. Some will argue that you can warm up with a few belts of liquor; at this point, that may be just what your game needs.

TIP *If you have to play with an orange ball because you'd lose a white one in the snow, this may be a scorecard you end up framing.*

"Seriously, why is there even a full set of clubs in my bag?"

THE SHORT PITCH

Somewhere in hell there's a golf course where every shot is fifty-five yards from the hole. And you know as you stand over the tee that there is no way you're gonna get that little ball anywhere close. Accept this. And then swing harder than your instincts tell you is right because, as Albert Einstein and Dr. Ruth said, "Never up, never in."

BE YOUR OWN WORST CRITIC

Nobody likes to be criticized. So really get down on yourself when you're playing poorly. After all, if you're not playing like you think you should, you deserve it. Be vocal. Work yourself up. Encourage other people to join in. You'll lower your self-esteem. You'll look insane. You'll play badly. It's that simple!

And hey! If you want to look really pathetic, call yourself by name. (Say your own name as you practice the following examples.)

1. "Oh, come on, [name]!"

2. "What is your problem, [name]?!"

3. "That's it, [name]! Real smart!"

4. "Why do you keep doing that, [name]?!"

5. "[Naaaaaaaaaaaaaaaaaaaaaaaaaaame]!"

"Stupid! Stupid (name)!"

SWEARING

Anybody who claims to have never said a bad word on a golf course is a #@*%ing liar!!

Anyway . . .

Swearing is important because it tells your fellow golfers that you are nowhere near as bad as that last shot says you are. Swearing is like lying: The more you do it, the better you will get at it. And once you start, it's a slippery slope.

Here are a few things you may want to swear at during a gentlemanly round of golf:

Your swing, your ball, your clubs, trees, water hazards, bunkers, the wind, birds, the ground, the sun, the people behind you, the people in front of you, the people in front of them, the people you work with, old women, planes, sticks, rocks, divots, leaves, ball marks on the green, goose turds, Jerry, the time, the rain, the cold, the heat, greenskeepers, the marshall, your shoes, squirrels, pin placement, dew, sprinklers, and coyotes.

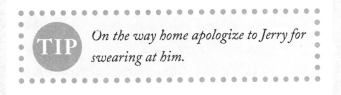

TIP *On the way home apologize to Jerry for swearing at him.*

FIGHT WITH THE MARSHALL

You'll know right away if the marshall is a good cop or a bad cop. Assume he's a bad cop. Here's a retired guy with a nagging wife at home who needs someone to take his frustrations out on. And you're in his way.

He'll probably use his limited power to demand that you stick to the cart path, even though it hasn't rained in weeks. Follow his instructions to the letter—until you can no longer see him.

Granted, it may get a little sticky at the turn when he asks why four of you are playing out of one cart and your answer is, "Because the other one is stuck in a sand trap." Which, by the way, is off the path.

But oh, what a proud moment when it escalates to the point where the yelling and swearing get you kicked off the course. And don't you want to hear this in thirty years? "Hey, Grandpa, tell me about the time you got banned from that par-three course for trying to shove a bag of tees up an old man's butt."

"Grandpa, tell us about the time you ran over the course marshall with your golf cart."

LIE

It's not fair that your wife is out working or at home with the kids while you're taking a day off to play golf. So don't tell her. And if she asks, lie. Treat playing golf like cheating on your wife. It will make the whole day feel a little dirty. A completely unnecessary strain on your marriage can only add strokes to your game.

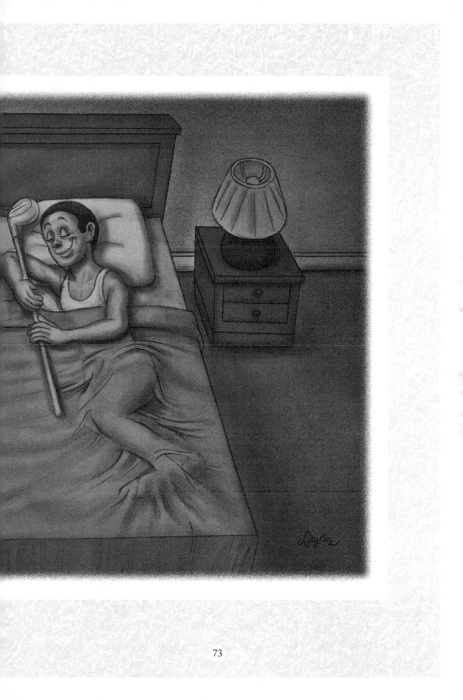

CHEAT

Cheating—or "the quiet shot," as I like to call it—is a wonderful way to wreck a bad score. Because we know deep down that if we hadn't kicked that ball away from that tree on the tenth fairway when the other guys weren't looking, we wouldn't have posted a low score.

It's hollow. It's not real. And instead of enjoying the after-game stories at the nineteenth hole, we're sitting on our shame-filled butts drinking an ice-cold bottle of guilt.

Hey! Listen! Never be ashamed of your real score. If you had to climb six fences and lost twenty-one balls, the 73 on your scorecard is not going to ring true. Besides, anybody can shoot a 73. They do it every week on television. It takes a lot more work to post a 138. Be proud of it!

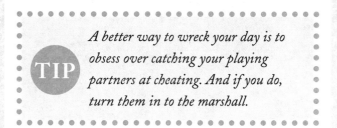

TIP

A better way to wreck your day is to obsess over catching your playing partners at cheating. And if you do, turn them in to the marshall.

SO, YOU WANT TO PLAY FOR MONEY

Here's an easy way to ruin a perfectly enjoyable game of golf: Put some money on the next hole. Any pleasure or relaxation you were enjoying is over. It's all business now. It doesn't have to be a lot of money, either. Because the moment you and your lifelong best friend put a nickel on the next hole, it's on! Sit back and watch, because the wheels are about to fall off.

Golf has nothing to do with it anymore. It's about winning money.

Of course, money is not the only thing you can bet. After you've lost eleven "double or nothing"s in a row, you can always bet your car or the deed to your house. What's the worst that could happen? Hey, the kids have been nagging you for a long time to take them camping.

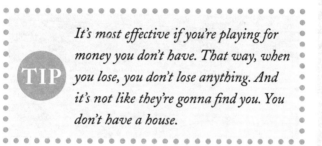

TIP *It's most effective if you're playing for money you don't have. That way, when you lose, you don't lose anything. And it's not like they're gonna find you. You don't have a house.*

WATER

Be it off the tee, in the middle of the fairway, or around the green, when you are in front of water, always use an inferior ball. Sure a new, unmarked ball with perfect aerodynamics would give you the best chance of success for clearing this hazard. But that's like wanting a professional to pack your parachute. Why lose a good ball?

Take out one of those faded, scuffed, no-name balls with a smile on it and do the best you can with it. Use a range ball if you've got one.

You'll be happy when it goes into the water. You'll secretly applaud yourself for having had the foresight to switch balls.

Congratulations! With one magic swing of your club you've added two more strokes to your score.

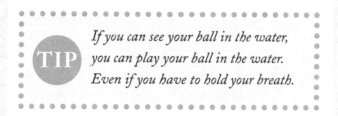

> **TIP**
> *If you can see your ball in the water, you can play your ball in the water. Even if you have to hold your breath.*

LESSONS

#@$#* lessons!!

They cost a lot, and they're too much like work. Golf isn't supposed to be work. Golf is what you want to be doing when you're *at* work.

And why should you go broke trying to execute what some snotty pro is teaching you when you can simply go back to "the way I've always done it" for free?

And who are these "golf pros" anyway? Unless the instructor's first name is a type of man-eating cat and his last name is where my ball goes most of the time, I don't want to learn from him. If they were really pros they'd be playing on Sunday. Which they're not. They're

con men out to destroy your "unique" swing.
Don't let them.

But let's say that for some strange reason
you do try some of the things a pro teaches you
and your game does start to improve. Don't
panic! You can get "your game" back on track
with one simple "swing thought": Lift your
head.

SAND TRAPS

I have no idea how to get out of a sand trap, and neither should you. Sand traps are wonderful opportunities for piling on the strokes. Just choke up on the club, instruct your playing partners to get out of the line of fire, and start whacking. If you do it right, the trap should look like downtown Baghdad when you finally climb out of it.

PLAYING IN A TIME CRUNCH

Nothing takes the leisure out of a round of golf quite like trying to play a five-hour game in an hour and a half. Especially if the course is crowded. Try to schedule your golf game for the same day as your child's birthday party or your anniversary.

You'll have knots in your neck the size of softballs as you contemplate the trouble you're going to be in, because at this very moment there's a crowd of people waiting on you so they can "light the candles" and you're only on hole number twelve.

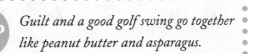

TIP *Guilt and a good golf swing go together like peanut butter and asparagus.*

GOLF ETIQUETTE

If the group behind you hits a ball near you, no matter how close it comes, make a big deal over it. Drop to the ground like you were shot at. Then calmly walk over to their ball, line it up, and hit it back at them. Believe me, you'll be amazed at how straight and long this shot will go. The feud is on. If the course

TIP

If you've listened to what I've said and are ready to apply these guidelines and principles, you're going to be hitting a lot of really bad shots. So I suggest you yell "Fore!" after every swing to ensure that the people in front of you stay safe.

gets backed up in front of you and there's obviously going to be a confrontation, do the honorable thing: Trade shirts with Jerry and blame it on him.

SUPERSTITION IS THE WAY

If you have rituals, tics, or superstitions, keep them up. Some people look down on rituals. They have all these incredibly focused, scientific results that prove, without a doubt, that superstitions don't work. These "people" insist that things like skill and determination will defeat not changing one's underwear during a lucky streak.

Are you kidding me?

A lot of brave men and women fought in a lot of wars to protect your right to delude yourself however you want to!

I don't care if you rub your driver on your stomach before you swing because you think it'll bring you luck. Do it! So what if you continue to hit only 7 percent of your fairways? Keep doing it. If it starts to work, then stop.

The opposite of superstition and luck is skill and practice—which one do you trust to get you into the triple digits?

"Does this work on women?"

KISS MY PUTT

There are many ways to "three-putt" or better. Here are my favorites:

1. When in doubt about the speed of a putt, always leave it short. Unless it's uphill. Then hit it past the hole so that your next two putts can be downhill.

2. Keep reminding yourself that this two-foot putt you're lining up is worth the same number of strokes as that 280-yard drive you hit a few holes ago. This is a great way to bring on the yips.

3. In the split second before you putt the ball, suddenly decide to try a new putting

technique. The more radical the change, the better.

If you manage to leave each green having no clue about what you did wrong, you are way ahead of the game.

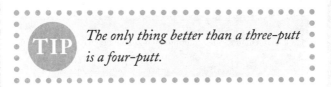

The only thing better than a three-putt is a four-putt.

RENTAL CLUBS SPELL SUCCESS

When you buy a nice set of clubs that have been fitted to you and you use them more than once, you run the risk of starting to strike the ball consistently. Shame on you. That's why *rental clubs spell success.* So if you have your own clubs, leave them in the car.

What should you look for in rental clubs? The second you see them you should be saying to yourself, "When did I have my last tetanus shot?"

1. The head of the putter should look like it's been used to build a tree house.

2. You want to be worried that the head will come flying off when you swing your

nine-iron. You can base this worry on the fact that it happened to your eight-iron two holes back.

3. You're not sure whether to hit your driver or donate it to a museum.

Put them all in the same bag and you've got yourself a beautiful train wreck, my friend.

My fellow golfers. The key to getting the least out of your golf game is found in the preceding hallowed pages. Now it's up to you to get out there and stink.

THE END

ABOUT THE AUTHORS

JEFF FOXWORTHY is the largest-selling comedy-recording artist in history, a multiple Grammy Award nominee, and the bestselling author of more than twenty books, including his Redneck Dictionaries. He is the host of the Fox television series *Are You Smarter Than a 5th Grader?* Jeff also starred in all three *Blue Collar Comedy Tour* movies, which have sold more than eight million copies and are some of the highest-rated movies in Comedy Central history. His syndicated weekly radio show, *The Foxworthy Countdown,* is carried in more than 220 markets across the United States. A Georgia native, he lives with his wife and two daughters in Atlanta.

BRIAN HARTT is a veteran writer and producer of many hit comedies, including *The Kids in the Hall, MADtv,* and *The Jamie Kennedy Experiment.* He also worked with Jeff on *Blue Collar TV.* He lives in Los Angeles with his wife and their two children.